Contents

ISBN 1-84146-178-4
Groovy website: www.cgpbooks.co.uk
Jolly bits of clipart from CorelDRAW
Printed by Elanders Hindson, Newcastle upon Tyne.

Doing the Tests

There are **two sets** of practice papers in this pack.
Each set has:

Writing Test   **35 marks**
15 minutes for planning
45 minutes for writing

(you'll need some lined paper to write your answer —
2 sheets should be enough if you write on both sides)

Reading Test   **50 marks**
15 minutes for reading
45 minutes for answering the questions

Spelling and Handwriting Test   **25 marks**
15 minutes

*Get someone to read out the
spelling tests for you. They're on
pages 60 and 61 of this book.*

In the exams you write your answers for the Reading and Spelling & Handwriting tests in the question book. If you want to do these practice tests more than once then write on a separate piece of paper.

Follow all the instructions

1) **Plan** your writing before you start. For the writing test, use the planning sheets — make sure you know how you're going to finish.

2) The most important thing is to **understand** the questions.
Read everything really **carefully** to be sure you're doing what they want.

ENGLISH
KEY STAGE 2

Writing Paper 1

45 MINUTES

Levels 3 – 5

Writing Test
Instructions and Planning Sheets

You must choose **one** piece of writing from these four:
1. **Mountain Village** is a leaflet
2. **Tree Lover** is a letter
3. **Lost** is a short story
4. **The Boxes** is a short story

Use the planning sheet to help you organise your ideas.

You have **15 minutes** to think about what to write and note down ideas.

You will then be given some lined paper to write on.

You will have 45 minutes to do your writing.

1. *Mountain Village*

A new *Mountain Village* centre has been opened in the Lake District, to give people the chance to enjoy outdoor activities.

The centre needs a leaflet, to tell people about everything that you can see and do. It should try to **persuade** them to go to the centre.

Some pictures to go in the leaflet have already been drawn.

You have to write the words to go in the leaflet.

You should think about:

■ reasons why people should go to the centre

■ what there is to see and do

■ other useful information

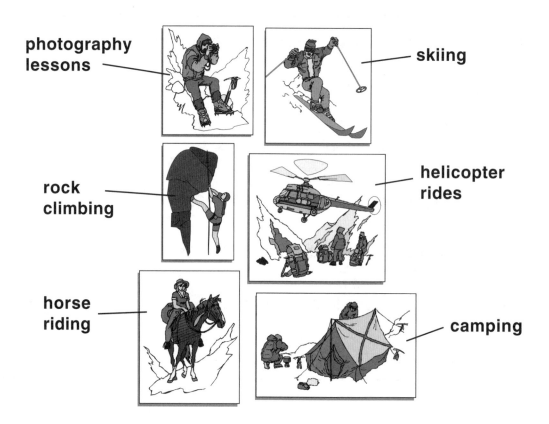

photography lessons

skiing

rock climbing

helicopter rides

horse riding

camping

Planning Notes

Write **very brief notes** to help you plan ideas for your writing.

The notes will not be marked.

Remember that the leaflet has to **inform** people about the centre and **persuade** them to go there.

Think about:
- what information you should include
- how you will persuade people to go

NOTE: You WON'T get any marks for drawing pictures or decoration. If you want the leaflet to have more pictures, just write brief notes to say what the pictures would show.

2. *Tree Lover*

Here are some facts about trees:

- trees provide a home for birds, insects and squirrels
- the roots of trees hold soil together and stop it being washed away
- many trees have nuts or berries which provide food for birds and animals
- the leaves of trees put oxygen into the air for us to breathe
- trees are very strong and don't blow down except in very high winds

A letter has been printed in a local newspaper:

Dear Editor

My house has a big garden full of trees. I am very worried that they will be making the air bad. I don't want them to scare the beautiful birds and squirrels away. They must have really big roots which will loosen the soil — what if it washes away? I am terrified every time my children play near them because they might lean on a tree and push it over.
Can anyone tell me what I ought to do?

Yours sincerely,

Jane Doggart

23 Spider Lane, Flyton, FL9 2XY

Write a letter directly to **Jane Doggart**.
Persuade her why she is wrong about trees, using the tree facts and any other information you know.

Planning Notes

Write **very brief notes** to help you plan ideas for your writing.

The notes will not be marked.

Think about:
- *how to **start** the letter*
- *the best way to **organise** your points*
- *how to make your points as **clearly** as possible so that Jane Doggart realises that she is wrong about trees*
- *how to **finish** your letter*

Remember, you're trying to persuade Jane Doggart that she is wrong about trees.

3. *Lost*

Write a short story with the title *Lost*.

You have to decide:

- how and why the characters have become lost

- how the characters feel when they are lost

- what they try to do

Planning Notes

Write **very brief notes** to help you plan ideas for your writing.

The notes will not be marked.

Before you start, you might want to note your ideas down in this table.

The characters in your story	
When the story takes place	
Where the story takes place	

Use your notes to help you plan out the story.

Think about:
- how the story starts
- what happens in the story
- how the story finishes

4. *The Boxes*

*I couldn't believe my eyes! On the doorstep were two
big boxes, full to the brim. I just didn't know what to do.*

Write a short story using this idea.

You have to decide:

- what was in the boxes
- what you decided to do with the boxes
- what happened

Planning Notes

Write **very brief notes** to help you plan ideas for your writing.

The notes will not be marked.

Think about:

- *how the story starts*
- *what happens in the story*
- *when and where the story takes place*
- *what the characters are like*
- *how the story finishes*

IMPORTANT: Spend 15 minutes reading the booklet 'Flying High' before you try answering the questions —
you'll find it after P28. If you decide to detach the booklet, fold the staple back so you don't spike yourself!

ENGLISH
KEY STAGE 2

Reading
Paper 1
45 MINUTES

Levels
3 – 5

TOTAL SCORE

FIRST GO:

SECOND GO:

THIRD GO:

Reading Test
Flying High

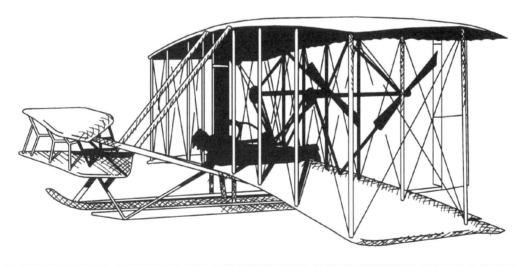

FIRST NAME

LAST NAME

SCHOOL

How to Answer the Questions

This test includes different questions for
you to answer in different ways.

short answer questions

You'll get a single line to write your answer,
so just write a single word or a short phrase.

medium answer questions

These questions are followed by several lines.
Use more words or sentences in your answer.

long answer questions

You'll be given more lines to write your answer on.
Use full sentences to explain your opinion in detail.

multiple choice questions

To answer these, you just have to ring the correct answer.
Here is an example of a multiple choice question:

The 'funny bone' is also called

| the hilarious | the hysterical | the humerus | the ridiculous |

Marks

The boxes in the margins have the maximum number
of marks for each question written underneath.

Don't do anything until you are told to start work.
Work through the questions until you are told to stop.
Use your reading booklet whenever you need to.

> # You will have 15 minutes reading time
> # followed by 45 minutes to do the test.

SECTION 1

These questions are about *Wonderful Wings.*

1.   On pages 4 and 5 you can find out how birds fly.
       Birds get the lift to take off from

| jumping from the ground | dropping their wings | jumping off trees | flapping their wings |

1 mark

2.   The difference between small and larger birds flying is that

| big birds have to fly lower in the sky | the larger the bird the more it has to flap | the larger the bird the less it has to flap | small birds can fly faster |

1 mark

3.   When large birds are flying, they look like they are

| shooting through the air | hanging in the air | looking for somewhere nice to land | resting their wings |

1 mark

4.   Planes, gliders and birds all fly in a similar way using

| flapping to get them into the sky | specially shaped wings | pockets of rising air | light materials |

1 mark

5.   The information on pages 4 and 5 tells us how birds, planes and gliders fly.
       Below are facts about birds, planes and gliders.
       Match each fact to what it's describing by writing A, B or C in the boxes.
       Some statements need to be matched with **two** letters, others only need **one**.

A bird   **B** plane   **C** glider

| | It pushes air downwards to keep it in the air. |

| | It is made of light materials and is streamlined. |

| | It needs strong, powerful wings to take off. |

| | The thrust of its engine drives it forwards. |

| | It flies downwards looking for pockets of air to lift it up. |

2 marks

6.   The title of pages 4-5 is **Wonderful Wings**.

Why did the author choose this title?

....

....

....

2 marks

7.   Why are planes made of light materials?

....

....

....

2 marks

8.   The different types of flier described on page 5
     use different methods of staying in the air.
     Fill in the information missing from this table.

Flier	How it flies
....	**Thrust from the engine lifts its weight.**
....	....
Bird	....

4 marks

9.   Look at the sections on page 4 called *Wonderful Wings*
     and *How a plane flies*.

     How do you know that the section called *Wonderful Wings* is more
     important than *How a plane flies*?
     Write down **two** ways.

     1. ....

         ....

     2. ....

         ....

2 marks

10. *Instead it looks like it is hanging in the air.*
    In reality, the seagull **isn't** hanging from anything.
    Why do you think the writer chose to use the word *'hanging'*?

    ....

    ....

    ....

2 marks

11. Write down **three** facts about planes.

    1. ....

    2. ....

    3. ....

1 mark

12. Why is the information in the fact boxes
    easier to find than in the introduction?

    ....

    ....

1 mark

SECTION 2

These questions are about *First Flight.*

1.   What time of day does the flight in the poem take place?

....

1 mark

2.   The poem starts with the words '*Turning and twisting*'.
         Why do you think it starts with these words?

....

....

1 mark

3.   Write down two things that happen in the last two verses of the poem.

         1.   ....

               ....

         2.   ....

               ....

2 marks

4.   The word '*turning*' is used in the poem to mean '*flying*'.
     Write down four other words for 'flying' that are used in the poem.

     1.   ....

     2.   ....

     3.   ....

     4.   ....

2 marks

5.   How is the last verse different from the rest of the poem?

     ....

     ....

1 mark

6.   In the third verse, the plane's trail is described as: '*a slug's trail on a
     leaf of clover*'. What does this image tell you about the plane's trail?

     ....

     ....

     ....

     ....

1 mark

7.   What do you think the writer means by '*happy but sad*'?

....

....

....

....

8(a)   In the first verse of the poem, the writer uses the word
        '*patchwork*' to describe the fields. Explain what this means.

....

....

(b)   Why do you think the writer chose the word '*patchwork*'?

....

....

....

....

These questions are about *Famous Fliers.*

1. *'Everyone is excited...'* *'The observers watch, amazed.'*
   The Wright Brothers' Flight is written in the present tense.
   Why do you think it is written in the present tense?

   ....

   ....

   ....

   ....

1 mark

2. Draw a line matching these facts to the famous fliers.

   | Orville and Wilbur Wright |

   flew from Calais to Dover

   won a prize of £10 000

   | John Alcock and Arthur Whitten Brown |

   made the first flight in history

   damaged the plane during landing

   flew for more than 16 hours

   | Louis Bleriot |

   made the flight in December

3 marks

3.   Look at these statements from the texts.
      Decide whether they are **fact** or **opinion**.
      Write 'FACT' or 'OPINION' next to the statement.
      One has been filled in as an example.

                                                                    OPINION

      Alcock and Brown were the greatest fliers of all time.   ....

      Orville Wright made the first powered flight in history.   ....

      The sea must have been dark and frightening to fly over.   ....

      What an incredible day.   ....

      The plane sometimes darted up to ten feet in the air.   ....

      Alcock and Brown were national heroes.   ....

3 marks

4.   Write down **two** strange ideas for flying machines which
      are mentioned in the introduction to *Famous Fliers*.

      1.   ....

      2.   ....

2 marks

5. Look at *The Flight of Daedalus and Icarus*.
    Write down **two** words the writer uses to describe the wings Daedalus made.
    For each word, write down **why** you think the writer chose it.

    word: ....

    why the writer chose it: ....

    ....

    word: ....

    why the writer chose it: ....

    ....

2 marks

6.   At the end of '*The Flight of Daedalus and Icarus*', it says:
      '*Some people think that this story shows*
      that human beings shouldn't try to fly.'
      Why do you think people might think this? Explain your answer fully.

      ....

      ....

      ....

      ....

2 marks

These questions are about the whole booklet.

1. The different texts in this booklet have been written by different people for different purposes.

    Draw **one** line matching each text to someone **most likely** to have written it.

Wonderful Wings	someone writing for a newspaper
First Flight	someone who wants to tell you how amazing flying feels
The Flight of Daedalus and Icarus	an ornithologist (someone who studies birds)
Bleriot crosses the Channel	someone who's not sure if people should fly

2 marks

2.	Some people are afraid of flying.

Explain **why** they might change their minds if they read this booklet.
Use evidence from **all parts** of the booklet.
Answer as fully as you can.

....

....

....

....

....

....

....

3 marks

Spelling and Handwriting
Snakes

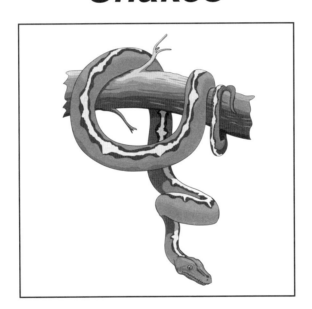

FIRST NAME

LAST NAME

SCHOOL

Snakes

There are thousands of .... types of snake.

The .... type of snake is the boa constrictor,

.... can grow to over ten metres long.

Boa constrictors are .... of eating animals as

big as pigs. When they .... their prey they

wrap around it until it is completely .... Then

they swallow it ....

Snakes look ...., but they are

.... very rough to touch. As they increase in

.............................., they have to shed their skin because it is

so tough.

Snakes don't .... attack people unless they

(or their nests) are stepped on. Some people

.... that you can suck the poison out if

.... is bitten by a snake. This is not true

because the venom travels far too ....

through the blood vessels.

There are three .... of snake in Britain. These
are adders (also known as vipers), grass snakes and smooth
snakes. Dry heathlands are the best ....
habitats for British snakes, but many now find
.... homes in railway embankments, road
verges, churchyards and golf courses.

Adders are found all over Britain and are our only snakes
with a poisonous bite, but this is .... fatal
to humans.

Grass snakes are .... good swimmers and
they feed mainly on amphibians such as toads, frogs,
newts and small fish.

Smooth snakes are less ...., living on
heathlands in Dorset, Hampshire and Surrey.

Spelling Mark

Handwriting

Here is a short paragraph that finishes the passage about snakes. Write it out very neatly in your own handwriting. You will be given a mark for your handwriting. Remember to make your writing as neat as possible, joining your letters if you can.

Most snakes live on land, but some live in the sea. Thirty-two species of sea snake have been identified in the waters around Australia. Due to their need to breathe air, they are usually found in shallow water, where they swim about on the bottom feeding on fish, fish eggs and eels.

_____

_____

_____

_____

_____

_____

_____

_____

_____

Handwriting Mark

ENGLISH
KEY STAGE 2

Writing

Paper 2

45 MINUTES

Levels

3 – 5

Writing Test

Instructions and Planning Sheets

You must choose **one** piece of writing from these four:

1. **Stop Press!** is an interview
2. **Special Delivery** is two diary entries
3. **I Couldn't Go Home** is a short story
4. **School Hero** is a short story

Use the planning sheet to help you organise your ideas.

You have **15 minutes** to think about what to write and note down ideas.

You will then be given some lined paper to write on.

You will have 45 minutes to do your writing.

1. *Stop Press!*

Imagine you've interviewed someone who's just done something interesting.

It could be an author, someone you know, or somebody who is famous.

You have to decide:

■ whom you have interviewed

■ what they did that was interesting

You have to write out the interview, with:

■ **the questions you asked**

■ **what the person said**

Write the questions and answers out like this:

Interviewer: *Why did you decide to write a story about a dragon?*

Author: *I like using my imagination to write about things that I've never seen. I like to create strange creatures, and imagine what would happen if they met ordinary people in the everyday world.*

Planning Notes

Write **very brief notes** to help you plan ideas for your writing.

The notes will not be marked.

Make brief notes about the things the person tells you.

Phrases you might want to use:

When did the...?   How long...?   Did they...?

What did you think about...?   Why did you...?

2. *Special Delivery*

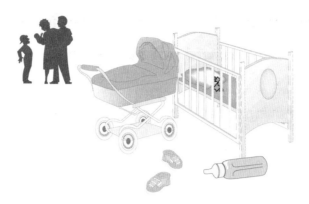

Imagine your parents had a new baby.
You had to give up your bedroom and help to look after the baby.

During this time, you kept a diary to write down the things
that happened and how you felt about the baby.

Write two diary entries:

■ the first written **just before** the new baby was born

■ the second written **after** the baby was born, and has come home

You have to think about:

■ things that will change around the house

■ your feelings about the baby

■ what the new baby is like

Planning Notes

Write **very brief notes** to help you plan ideas for your writing.

The notes will not be marked.

Make brief notes about the things that happened and how you felt.

*Remember, you have to write **two** entries in your diary.*

Before the baby was born...

After the baby was born...

3. *I Couldn't Go Home*

She was so ashamed. Her stomach felt like it was tied in knots. She knew she had to go home eventually, but if Dad was home, he'd see guilt written all over her face.

Write a short story using this idea.

You have to decide:

- what had happened

- who was involved

- why she didn't want to go home

Flying High

FLYING HIGH

Contents

INTRODUCTION

Since the beginning of time, people have always wanted to fly.
Nowadays, there are lots of ways to fly — in aeroplanes, gliders,
balloons and all sorts of other things.

Some people really enjoy flying.
Others find it frightening, especially the first time they do it.
The first people to fly were very brave.
A lot of people at the time thought they were mad to even try.
Nowadays, it's become something completely normal,
and most people don't think twice about it.

In this booklet we will look at flying
in three different ways.

- *facts about how things fly in 'Wonderful Wings'*

- *the wonderful feeling of flying for the first time
  in a poem called 'First Flight'*

- *three accounts of early aeroplane flights and an
  old legend about flying in a section called
  'Famous Fliers'*

Wonderful Wings

The easiest way to learn about flight is by watching birds.
Birds get most of their lift from flapping their wings.
The wings push the air around the bird downwards, which lifts
the bird up. As long as the bird keeps flapping, it can move
through the air without dropping down again. If the bird stops
flapping, it will slow down and start to drop.

In order to take off and stay up in the air, birds need strong,
powerful wings. But if you watch a bird with big wings, like a
seagull, and a bird with small wings, like a sparrow, you will see
that the seagull doesn't have to flap as often as the sparrow.
Instead it looks like it is hanging in the air.

This is because the seagull is gliding.   A bird's wing is specially
shaped so that the top part is slightly curved. When the bird is
gliding, the air underneath the wing lifts it up, so it can fly for
long distances without much effort. This how people fly using
hang-gliders and glider planes.

How a plane flies

Like birds, planes use specially shaped wings to move through
the air. But to get up there, they need huge engines.
The engines need to thrust the plane forward along the runway
extremely fast to lift the weight of the plane into the air.
This is why planes are made of light materials and streamlined
to stop the air dragging them back.

How Birds Fly

- A bird flies by flapping its wings or by gliding.

- When flapping its wings, the wings push air downwards, which pushes the bird up.

- When gliding, the passing air lifts the bird up because of the shape of the wings.

How Aeroplanes Fly

- The wings are shaped so the passing air lifts the weight of the plane.

- The thrust of the engine pushes the plane forward.

How Gliders Fly

- Like aeroplanes' wings, the wings are specially shaped.

- Gliders fly slowly downwards, looking for pockets of rising air to take them back up.

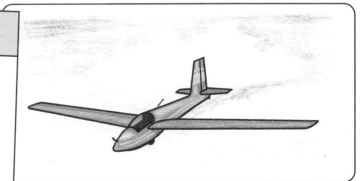

Living

With

Nature

CONTENTS

Introduction

People have always had an effect on nature. Since ancient times, we have kept animals as pets or in zoos. Until recently, few people thought about the effect this had on the animals. Nowadays, we have learned a lot more about how we can live alongside nature, without damaging it or the animals who share it with us.

In this booklet, you will read a story about how the Emperor of China became friends with a songbird in *The Emperor and the Nightingale*. Then you will read an interview with Pete Lewis, who works to raise awareness about the effect people have on the environment, in *An Interview with a Conservationist*. Lastly, you will read about some of the rare animals who are under threat in the wild, and how people are trying to protect and breed them in zoos and reserves in *Animals at Risk*.

The Emperor and the Nightingale

The Emperor of China was a proud and strong man. The people he ruled lived in terror of his fierce temper. His advisers were all afraid of him.

One day, however, things were to change completely. The Emperor was walking in his garden, with his advisers following behind him. Suddenly he stopped. He could hear the most marvellous music drifting lazily through the wind. It made him think of wonderful hot summer days doing nothing, of lying in the shade with a cold drink. The Emperor closed his eyes, and for the first time in his life, he felt at peace with the world.

Almost immediately, they snapped open again.

"Where is that music coming from?" he asked his astonished advisers.

"It is the song of a nightingale," answered one, trembling with fear.

"Bring the nightingale to me," he ordered, enchanted, and the advisers scurried off to look for the bird in the large palace gardens.

Finally they found it, a small, pretty bird, and brought it to where the Emperor stood waiting.

"This is the nightingale, my lord," said the bravest of the advisers.

"Bring it to my room so it can sing for me," commanded the Emperor.

And so the nightingale was brought into the palace, where it would flutter through the many rooms singing sweetly for the Emperor. Whenever the Emperor felt tired, or when he was bored, or even when he couldn't get to sleep at night, the nightingale would sing to him.

Now the Emperor was very pleased with the nightingale, but in his heart he was also worried. What would happen if the bird flew away? It might never come back, and then he would never hear it sing again.

He tried not to think about this, but the thought stayed with him, twisting itself into his mind until he couldn't think of anything else. Eventually, after a sleepless night, he summoned his goldsmith, and commanded him to make a cage for the nightingale.

The goldsmith worked all day and long into the night, and soon he had made a beautiful gold cage, inlaid with emeralds and rubies. He brought it to the Emperor.

By this time, the nightingale had grown used to living in the palace, and had become quite happy to sit on the Emperor's desk and even on his shoulder. That evening, the nightingale was sitting on the desk singing cheerfully, when the Emperor suddenly lunged forward and caught it in his hands. The Emperor laughed happily as he put the bird safely into the cage. He would never be short of music now.

But the nightingale grew sad, trapped in the golden cage. It could no longer fly through the palace or follow the Emperor around. Instead it had become a prisoner. Soon it grew so sad that it didn't have the energy to sing any more, and did nothing but hop mournfully round its cage.

The Emperor became furious. "Ungrateful creature!" he raged. "Why should I waste my time on a bird that won't sing?"

His advisers became worried. Life at the Court had become much happier since the Emperor had discovered the song of the nightingale. "If the nightingale will not sing, then the Emperor will grow angry with us." They sat and thought for a while, and then came up with a plan. That night they sent for the goldsmith.

The next day, the Emperor sat in his throne room when the goldsmith entered, carrying a large box. "Your Excellency," he began. "I bring you a gift from your trusted advisers."

The Emperor waved him to open the box, and the goldsmith carefully lifted out a golden cage, even more beautiful than the last one. This time, however, there was something else inside — a mechanical bird, with rubies for eyes and beautiful feathers of real gold. The goldsmith put it on a table beside the nightingale's cage. Compared to the new golden bird, the real nightingale looked dull and dirty.

The Emperor clapped his hands. "This new bird is much more beautiful than the old one."

The goldsmith smiled, and took a large golden key out of his pocket, which he turned ten times in the base of the new cage. As soon as he had finished, the golden bird suddenly raised its head and began to sing, loudly and clearly.

The Emperor was amazed. "This is wonderful," he said. The mechanical nightingale ended its song, and the advisers applauded, but the goldsmith stepped forward and wound the key again. Again the golden bird began to sing, exactly the same song, just as sweetly as before.

The Emperor was delighted. "This bird will sing for me whenever I want."

The advisers applauded again, and secretly congratulated themselves on their cleverness. But the nightingale sat sadly in its cage, while the clockwork bird sang the same song over and over again.

The nightingale had stopped eating because it was so sad, and soon it was so thin that the golden cage could no longer keep it trapped. One night, while the Emperor was listening to his mechanical bird, the nightingale slipped through the bars and flew away through the darkness, without anyone noticing.

Meanwhile, the Emperor still loved his new toy. "This bird is much finer than the old one," he said to himself. "It sings all the time, and never changes its song. The old bird didn't even sing a proper tune most of the time, but this one does. Its golden feathers are much finer than real feathers, and it always does what I command."

A year passed, and the Emperor had become much older and frailer. The song of the mechanical bird no longer seemed fresh and exciting to him. Every time he wound the key, the song came back exactly the same as the last time.

Soon he became ill. "Listen to the song of the golden bird," his advisers told him. "Surely it will make you feel young and happy again."

But the Emperor grew angry. "I'm bored with this stupid machine!" he shouted, sweeping the cage onto the floor with his hand. The mechanical bird fell off its perch and landed on the floor with a crunch, smashing into pieces. Tiny bits of gold and rubies scattered everywhere, leaving only a heap of cogs and springs. The clockwork bird was broken beyond repair.

The Emperor's advisers ran away, horrified. The Emperor stood, looking down at the broken machine. "It was only a toy," he thought to himself. "But I used to listen to a real nightingale."

Quickly, he hurried to his rooms, and strode to the old cage. "Sing to me, nightingale," he commanded. But the nightingale was gone. The Emperor let out a great howl.

"All this time I have been listening to a machine, and I kept the nightingale in a cage. Now it has gone, and it is all my fault. I shouldn't have treated it so badly." Sorry for what he had done, the Emperor sat down and wept for the nightingale.

Weeks passed and the Emperor grew ill. In front of him, his advisers acted concerned, and asked if they could do anything for him. Each time the Emperor answered,

"Find the nightingale, and ask it to come and sing to me once more." The advisers promised that they would look for the bird. But behind the Emperor's back, they did nothing, and whispered to each other that he was dying.

The Emperor grew sicker and sicker. His advisers said to each other, "Let us leave him. In the morning he will be dead, and we will have a new ruler." So they left the tired Emperor alone on his bed with his eyes closed. The wind blew softly through the windows, disturbing the wind chimes that hung there. The Emperor sighed at the sound of the chimes, because they reminded him of the nightingale's song. He could almost hear it again, filling the room with a beautiful sound. The sound continued, and the Emperor sighed again, as a peaceful feeling came over him. He opened his eyes.

There beside him sat the nightingale, singing happily. The Emperor was overjoyed. "Thank you for coming back to sing, my friend," he said, offering the bird some water on his finger.

In the morning, the advisers came hurrying to the palace, dressed in heavy, black robes and waddling like a troop of penguins. They were all expecting to find the Emperor dead, so they nearly jumped out of their skins when he flung open the door to his room and came out to greet them, very much alive and well. On his shoulder sat the nightingale, singing happily.

From that day on, the Emperor and the nightingale were always together, and the Emperor would never allow a cage anywhere near his palace. "The nightingale can go wherever it wants," he declared. "I will never try to keep it here against its will."

And that is the story of the Nightingale and the Emperor, and how they became true friends.

An Interview with a Conservationist

About Pete Lewis

Pete Lewis has been interested in the natural world since he was a boy.

He grew up in the Lake District, one of Britain's National Parks, and spent a lot of his childhood outdoors, doing plenty of walking, climbing and canoeing.

When he was 16, he decided that he wanted to become a conservationist. Conservationists are people who work to look after nature, and to preserve the environment as it is. He spends most of his time campaigning to stop developers from building on rare and important natural sites. He has travelled all over the world to see how conservation happens in different countries. Martin Bradshaw went to interview him.

Martin	*Why did you become interested in conservation?*
Pete	When I was young, living in the Lake District meant that I saw first-hand a beautiful part of the world that was being damaged. Every year, thousands of tourists would come to the area to climb the mountains and sail on the lakes. The problem was that many of the tracks up the mountain were being eroded because so many people were climbing them, and the speedboats on the lakes were disturbing the wildlife on the shores.

Martin	*And that made you feel guilty?*
Pete	Yes, it made me realise how much of an effect we can have on the natural world around us, even when we don't think we're affecting it at all.

Martin	*What did you do to get involved in conservation?*
Pete	I started writing letters to important people like politicians, even while I was at school. I also spent a lot of time finding out about the natural world. There are too many thoughtless and short-sighted people who don't think the things they do have any effect on the world around them.

Martin	*A big issue in conservation is zoos. What do you think about them?*
Pete	Well, zoos can be good and bad. I think it's cruel and wrong for people to take animals out of the wild to keep them in cages. In a perfect world, all animals should live in the wild, where they belong. Unfortunately, some animals are dying out, because of hunting, or because their habitats are being destroyed by things like deforestation. The only way to save animals like the giant panda is to protect them in zoos and to start breeding programmes. If zoos didn't look after pandas, they would have died out years ago.

Martin	*Lastly, can you explain to anyone who isn't sure, just why conservation is so important?*
Pete	Certainly. Conservation is important because without it many animals and plants we take for granted will disappear forever. It's all about thinking before we act — being aware that when we drop litter, or build new houses or even pick flowers, we could be damaging the world around us. But if we respect nature, then there's no reason why we can't avoid harming the environment, which will make the world a better place for all of us — people, animals and plants!

Glossary:

conservation = protecting the natural world

deforestation = cutting down and clearing forests to make space for farming or for land to build on

habitat = the natural home of an animal

eroded = worn away

<u>Animals at Risk</u>

Many animals around the world are endangered.
Without protection from hunters or from changes to
their habitats, some species of animal could die out
completely in the next few years. Animals like elephants
are hunted for the ivory in their tusks, while others are
hunted for their skins.

These animals should be protected in the wild, but often
they are still in danger from poachers — people who hunt
animals against the law. That's why some experts think
the best way to protect rare animals is in zoos, where
they can be kept safe from poaching. They can also be
bred in zoos, so that when the number of animals has
increased, some of them can be released back into the
wild. This has already happened with animals like the red
wolf, in a project described on the next page.

The Red Wolf Returns

Red wolves are back! These rare and wonderful animals used to live all over the South and West of America. Unfortunately, they started to die out completely because people were shooting them. I think a lot of people thought that they were dangerous just because they were wolves.

I think wolves are a bit like sharks — they scare people. As soon as anyone says 'wolf' or 'shark' people think of stupid horror films.

That's why some people want to hunt them down. Now, sadly, there are only a few wild red wolves left.

Recently, though, there's been some fantastic news. Red wolves have been reintroduced into reserves in North Carolina, South Carolina and Florida — and they seem to be doing really well. It's a great success for conservation, and hopefully more red wolves will be reintroduced in the future.

Here are some facts about three other animals at risk:

Giant Panda

The giant panda is a large mammal with a distinctive coat of white with black patches.   It lives in the bamboo forests of South-West China, eats plants and tends to live alone. These forests have largely been cut down to make way for villages and rice fields, leaving the panda without its main source of food. Now there are only about 300-400 Giant Pandas left in the world. Zoos that keep pandas work together on breeding programmes to try to encourage them to mate so that the population will increase.

Tiger

Tigers are large, powerful cats found in Asia. They have coats of yellow, black and orange stripes, and are keen hunters of birds, deer, cattle and reptiles. The largest type of tiger is the Siberian, which can grow up to four metres long! Tigers are becoming rarer nowadays, because many people hunt them for their skin. Many zoos have special breeding programmes for tigers, and in India there are now special reserves where tigers are protected.

Rhinoceros

The rhinoceros is a massive, thick-skinned mammal with one or two horns on its nose. It lives in Africa and Asia. It eats plants and tends to live on its own. Rhinos like to wallow in muddy pools in the heat of the day. In the last 30 years, many of the world's rhinos have been hunted for their horns. Some experts say that as many as 85% of the world's rhinos have been killed by poachers in that time.

First Flight

Turning and twisting
In the morning air,
My goggles misting
Over as we climb through the clouds,
The wind in our hair,
High above the patchwork fields
And the crowds
Gathered at the air show.

The pilot eases the control stick
And the plane yields
To his gentle touch,
Swooping low
Over the heads of the people,
Doing a loop-the-loop trick,
Narrowly missing a church steeple —
Not by much!

Up again,
Climbing high
Above yellow fields of grain,
And the plane rolls over,
Writing in the sky
With a gleaming trail of grey,
Like a slug's trail on a leaf of clover
Early in the day.

Then diving once more,
Landing back on the ground,
And walking away
Head spinning around,
Happy but sad,
Feeling different from before,
But not feeling bad:
I had my first flight today.

Famous Fliers

Since ancient times people have always wanted to fly. Over the years, all sorts of methods and machines have been tried, most of them unsuccessfully. Many famous inventors, like Leonardo Da Vinci, drew plans for machines that would allow human beings to fly. Other people actually built their machines and made attempts at flight.

Many people tried to copy the flight of birds, by building big flapping wings, but they usually ended up in a heap on the ground. Some had strange ideas, like using a whirling arm to launch their flying machines into the air, or even a gunpowder engine.

The first unpowered flight was in a hot-air balloon in 1783, but it wasn't until 1903 that the first powered flight in an aeroplane took place.

Look at the important flying dates below and then at the three short descriptions of famous flights. Then turn the page and read about the *Flight of Daedalus and Icarus*.

IMPORTANT FLYING DATES

1903	The Wright Brothers make the first powered flight on December 17th.
1909	Louis Bleriot flies across the English Channel from Calais to Dover.
1919	British pilots Alcock and Brown make the first flight across the Atlantic Ocean, from Newfoundland to Ireland.
1927	Charles Lindbergh flies solo from New York to Paris in his plane *The Spirit of St Louis*.

The Wright Brothers' Flight

It is a windy, freezing cold day in December. Orville and Wilbur Wright and several observers are huddled around a hot stove trying to keep warm. Everyone is excited and a little bit worried.

Feeling nervous, Orville climbs into position in their plane and prepares to attempt to take off. Struggling with the controls, Orville lifts the plane into the air. It runs just above the ground, sometimes darting up to about ten feet in the air, sometimes darting for the ground. The observers watch, amazed. After about a hundred feet it sinks to the ground. Orville has made the first powered flight in history. It has lasted twelve seconds. What an incredible day!

Bleriot crosses the Channel

July 25th, 1909. A tiny dot appeared in the sky over the English Channel. It was an aeroplane, carrying its builder, Louis Bleriot, over the 22 miles from Calais to Dover. The sea must have been dark and frightening to fly over.

After flying for nearly 40 minutes, Bleriot knew he had to land the plane. "At the risk of smashing everything, I cut the ignition at twenty metres. Now it was up to chance. The landing gear took it rather badly, the propellor was damaged, but my word, so what? I had crossed the Channel!"

Alcock and Brown's Amazing Flight

On June 14th 1919, Captain John Alcock and Lieutenant Arthur Whitten Brown took off from Newfoundland to fly over the Atlantic. During the flight, the two men were bitterly cold but they kept on going. Sixteen hours and twenty seven minutes after taking off, they landed at Clifden in Ireland.

When the two men arrived in London, they were national heroes. People thought they were the greatest fliers of all time. They even won a newspaper prize of £10,000 for their achievement!

The Flight of Daedalus and Icarus

This is an old Greek legend about an inventor called Daedalus. He had been brought to the island of Crete by the King to build a labyrinth. The King was so impressed that he refused to let Daedalus leave. Daedalus grew very unhappy, and he used to stand on the edge of the cliffs beside the King's palace, looking sadly out to sea towards his homeland.

One day as he stood there, he noticed the birds flying over the sea to Greece. "If they can fly away, why can't I?" he thought to himself.

Working quickly, he secretly made two pairs of wings out of feathers and wax, one pair for him and one for his son, Icarus. He made them very large so that they could support the heavy weight of a person, and put straps on them, so that they could wear them on their arms. Then he carefully curved each wing so that it was perfectly streamlined, exactly like a bird's wing.

Before they escaped, Daedalus warned his son not to fly too close to the Sun, because the wax in the wings would melt.

But as they soared into the air on their big and powerful wings, Icarus grew very excited.

"Look how high I can fly!" he shouted to his father. Daedalus called out to his son to be careful, but Icarus flew too high, and his wings melted in the bright sunlight, and so he fell into the sea and drowned.

Many people think that this story shows that human beings shouldn't try to fly.   It isn't natural for human beings to fly, after all. Or is it?

Planning Notes

Write **very brief notes** to help you plan ideas for your writing.

The notes will not be marked.

Think about:

■ *how the story starts*

■ *what happens in the story*

■ *when and where the story takes place*

■ *what the characters are like*

■ *how the story finishes*

4. *School Hero*

The next day at school, everyone heard about what had happened, and even people I didn't know were calling me a hero.

Write a short story using this idea.

You have to decide:

- what had happened

- why you were called a hero

- what happened next

Planning Notes

Write **very brief notes** to help you plan ideas for your writing.

The notes will not be marked.

Think about:

- *the build-up to the event*

- *how the story starts*

- *when and where the story takes place*

- *what the characters are like*

- *how the story finishes*

IMPORTANT: Spend 15 minutes reading the booklet 'Living With Nature' before you try answering the questions — you'll find it after P28. If you decide to detach the booklet, fold the staple back so you don't spike yourself!

ENGLISH
KEY STAGE 2

Reading
Paper 2
45 MINUTES

Levels
3 – 5

Reading Test
Living With Nature

FIRST NAME

LAST NAME

SCHOOL

How to Answer the Questions

This test includes different questions for
you to answer in different ways.

short answer questions

You'll get a single line to write your answer,
so just write a single word or a short phrase.

medium answer questions

These questions are followed by several lines.
Use more words or sentences in your answer.

long answer questions

You'll be given more lines to write your answer on.
Use full sentences to explain your opinion in detail.

multiple choice questions

To answer these, you just have to ring the correct answer.
Here is an example of a multiple choice question:

The 'funny bone' is also called

The humerus   **The hilarious**   **The hysterical**   **The ridiculous**

Marks

The boxes in the margins have the maximum number
of marks for each question written underneath.

Don't do anything until you are told to start work.
Work through the questions until you are told to stop.
Use your reading booklet whenever you need to.

You will have 15 minutes reading time
followed by 45 minutes to do this test.

SECTION 1

These questions are about *The Emperor and the Nightingale.*

Put a ring around the word or group of words that explains what happened in *The Emperor and the Nightingale* story.

1. The Emperor was the Emperor of

France	China	Japan	Greece

1 mark

2. The goldsmith made the Emperor a

towel rail	fire guard	crown	bird cage

1 mark

3. When the nightingale wouldn't sing, the Emperor called it

ungrateful creature	lovely birdy	feathered fiend	winged annoyance

1 mark

4. When the real nightingale came back to the Emperor, he

put it back in a cage in his room	ran away	wouldn't let cages near the palace	cried

1 mark

5. Why do you think the nightingale was sad? (page 6)

....

....

....

2 marks

6.   What did the Emperor feel when he first heard the nightingale sing?

....

....

2 marks

7.   What happened next in the story?

....

....

....

1 mark

8.   Find **two** parts of the story when the Emperor changes his mind.
      When are they?

1.   ....

      ....

2.   ....

      ....

2 marks

9.   *Meanwhile, the Emperor still loved his new toy.*
      Find **four** reasons in the story why the Emperor said he preferred the
      mechanical bird to the nightingale.

      1.   ....

            ....

      2.   ....

            ....

      3.   ....

            ....

      4.   ....

            ....

      4 marks

10.   The goldsmith turned the golden key ten times in the base of the new cage.
      What happened after he did this?

      ....

      ....

      1 mark

11.   After a year has passed in the story, the Emperor seems to be different.
      Find **three** clues in the story that show how he is different.

      1.   ....

           ....

      2.   ....

           ....

      3.   ....

           ....

2 marks

12.   How do you think the Emperor felt when he realised that the
      nightingale was gone?

      ....

      ....

      ....

2 marks

13.   On page 9, the author says that the Emperor's advisers were *like a troop of penguins.*
Explain why you think the author uses this image.

....

....

....

1 mark

14.   At the start of the story, the Emperor is selfish and cruel, but by the end he has become a much kinder and wiser person.
Do you agree with this opinion? (Circle yes or no.)

YES   *NO*

Explain your answer fully, using evidence from the story to help you.

....

....

....

....

....

3 marks

15.   The title of the story is *The Emperor and the Nightingale*.
      At the end of the story, the author uses the same words again, but this time
      they are swapped around so it's written as *the Nightingale and the Emperor*.
      Why do you think the author has made this change?

      ....

      ....

      ....

1 mark

16.   The story of *The Emperor and the Nightingale* is a fairy tale.
      Write down **one** way that it is different from other kinds of story.

      ....

      ....

      ....

1 mark

17.	Some fairy tales have messages behind the story.
	What do you think is the message of *The Emperor and the Nightingale*?
	Explain as fully as you can.

	....

	....

	....

	....

	....

	....

3 marks

SECTION 2

1.　Write down three **facts** from the interview with Pete Lewis.

1.　..46...................................

....

2.　...

....

3.　...

....

1 mark

2.　In the interview, Pete Lewis uses the words *thoughtless and short-sighted* to describe people who don't think they have an effect on the world around them.
These people aren't actually thoughtless or short-sighted.
Explain fully why you think he uses these words in the interview.

....

....

....

2 marks

3.　The interview gives several reasons why zoos can be a good or bad idea.
Has reading this information changed your mind about zoos?
(Circle yes or no.)

YES　　　　　*NO*

Give reasons to explain your answer.

....

....

....

2 marks

The questions on this page are about how the information is presented.

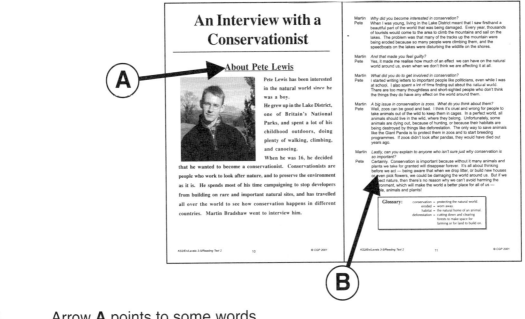

4.   Arrow **A** points to some words.
      Why have these words been made to stand out?

      ....

      ....

1 mark

5.   What does the letter **B** point to on the page?
      Circle the correct answer below.

      | a title | an interview | a bullet point | a bibliography |

1 mark

6.   What is a glossary?

....

....

....

1 mark

SECTION 3

1.   Find three similarities between **two** of the animals described.

     1.   ....

          ....

     2.   ....

          ....

     3.   ....

          ....

3 marks

2.   Which of the animals hunts birds, deer, cattle and reptiles?

                                        ....

1 mark

3.   In *The Red Wolf Returns*, the writer says, *"I think wolves are a bit like sharks."*
     In what ways does the article say wolves are like sharks?

     ....

     ....

     ....

2 marks

4. Look at the description of the rhinoceros and the piece called
    The Red Wolf Returns.

    How can you tell from the writers' styles that they were written by
    different people?

    ....

    ....

    ....

3 marks

5. This section is called *Animals at Risk.*

    Why do you think this title was chosen?

    ....

    ....

    ....

1 mark

SECTION 4

1.   Which of the texts in the booklet did you enjoy reading the most?

Explain your answer as fully as possible using evidence from all parts of the booklet.

....

....

....

....

....

....

3 marks

ENGLISH
KEY STAGE 2

Spelling and Handwriting Paper 2
15 MINUTES

Levels 3 – 5

Spelling and Handwriting
Aliens

FIRST NAME

LAST NAME

SCHOOL

Aliens

I had never been someone who believed in all that X-file stuff
about aliens. That was, of course, before last summer.

It was a hot day and the Sun was .... high
in the sky. It was the first week of the summer
.... and I was lying in the park.

I became .... of a rustling in the
.... of the trees. I sat up to see what was
going on. The .... were shaking and a faint
.... sound was coming from all around.
I was .... imagining things, but I thought I
could see eyes .... the trees. I stood up
and found I was now the only one in the park.

I .... a glimpse of my shadow and it was

changing. It was .... out like a puddle of water

across the park. My feet were .... to the spot

and when I tried to call out, my words came out so

.... they barely made a sound. A

.... thoughts rushed through my head as I

slowly looked up.

Directly above me was a .... huge jumbo jet,

just hovering. Now, I .... from my science

lessons that this is absolutely ...., but there it

was, just kind of sitting there.

As I watched, the jet changed .... into an

equally huge disc. From the centre of the disc a

.... began to emerge hoof-first!

Slowly but surely an entire cow appeared and continued to

descend .... to the ground. As soon as the

cow landed there was a blinding flash, after which the disc

disappeared, leaving me alone in the park with this

.... beast.

Spelling Mark

Handwriting

Here is a short paragraph that finishes the passage about aliens. Write it out very neatly in your own handwriting. You will be given a mark for your handwriting. Remember to make your writing as neat as possible, joining your letters if you can.

So, Mrs Sculder, that is why I've brought a cow into school with me and it's also why we'll all be leaving school now. The cow has told me of a wonderful place where humans are farmed before being sold as very cheap burgers. As the voice of the cow, I command you all to follow me.

_____

_____

_____

_____

_____

_____

_____

_____

_____

_____

Handwriting Mark [   ]

Answers

Answers — How to Mark Your Paper

It's **easy**. Use the answers on the following pages to mark each test.

When you've done a **complete** practice paper (Reading, Writing, Spelling and Handwriting Tests), use the table below to work out what your Reading level and your Writing level are.

For your **Reading level**, just look up your number of marks from the Reading Test. For your **Writing level**, add together half your marks in the Spelling Test (round up), your Handwriting score and the Writing Test score, and look that up.

LEVEL	Reading	Writing
3	10 → 17	19 → 30
4	18 → 30	31 → 38
5	31 → 50	39 → 50

To find your **overall level**, add together your Reading and Writing scores, and use this table:

LEVEL	Total Score
N	0 → 25
2	26 → 28
3	29 → 48
4	49 → 69
5	70 → 100

Important!

Getting a particular level on one of these practice papers is **no guarantee** of getting it in the real SAT — **but** it's a pretty good guide.

Spelling test — Instructions and Answers

This passage should be read out twice — a pause should be left after each **bold** word to give enough time to write in the answer. The whole Spelling test should take about 10 minutes.

Paper 1 — Snakes

There are thousands of **different** types of snake. The **largest** type of snake is the boa constrictor, **which** can grow to over ten metres long. Boa constrictors are **capable** of eating animals as big as pigs. When they **catch** their prey they wrap around it until it is completely **trapped**. Then they swallow it **whole**.

Snakes look **slippery**, but they are **actually** very rough to touch. As they increase in **length**, they have to shed their skin because it is so tough.

Snakes don't **usually** attack people unless they (or their nests) are stepped on. Some people **believe** that you can suck the poison out if **someone** is bitten by a snake. This is not true because the venom travels far too **quickly** through the blood vessels.

There are three **types** of snake in Britain. These are adders (also known as vipers), grass snakes and smooth snakes. Dry heathlands are the best **natural** habitats for British snakes, but many now find **suitable** homes in railway embankments, road verges, churchyards and golf courses.

Adders are found all over Britain and are our only snakes with a poisonous bite, but this is **rarely** fatal to humans.

Grass snakes are **surprisingly** good swimmers and they feed mainly on amphibians such as toads, frogs, newts and small fish.

Smooth snakes are less **common**, living on heathlands in Dorset, Hampshire and Surrey.

Spelling test — Instructions and Answers

This passage should be read out twice — a pause should be left after each **bold** word to give enough time to write in the answer. The whole Spelling test should take about 10 minutes.

Paper 2 — Aliens

I had never been someone who believed in all that X-file stuff about aliens. That was, of course, before last summer.

It was a hot day and the Sun was **still** high in the sky. It was the first week of the summer **holidays** and I was lying in the park.

I became **aware** of a rustling in the **leaves** of the trees. I sat up to see what was going on. The **hedges** were shaking and a faint **whistling** sound was coming from all around. I was **probably** imagining things, but I thought I could see eyes **amongst** the trees. I stood up and found I was now the only one in the park.

I **caught** a glimpse of my shadow and it was changing. It was **spreading** out like a puddle of water across the park. My feet were **anchored** to the spot and when I tried to call out, my words came out so **quietly** they barely made a sound. A **million** thoughts rushed through my head as I slowly looked up.

Directly above me was a **particularly** huge jumbo jet, just hovering. Now, I **know** from my science lessons that this is absolutely **impossible**, but there it was, just kind of sitting there.

As I watched, the jet changed **smoothly** into an equally huge disc. From the centre of the disc a **creature** began to emerge hoof-first!

Slowly but surely an entire cow appeared and continued to descend **gently** to the ground. As soon as the cow landed there was a blinding flash, after which the disc disappeared, leaving me alone in the park with this **exciting** beast.

Handwriting Mark Scheme

MARKS	1	2	3	4	5
handwriting is legible	✓	✓	✓	✓	✓
letters have correct shape and orientation		Mostly	✓	✓	✓
size and spacing of letters is consistent		Mostly	✓	✓	✓
letters are joined and parallel				Mostly	✓
stylistic features are used confidently					✓

The ticks shown here are the *minimum* needed to get the mark indicated.
E.g. If the letters are *not* joined or parallel, only *three* marks
may be given, even if stylistic features have been used.

Example awarded 5 marks

Most snakes live on land, but some live in the sea.

Example awarded 4 marks

Most snakes live on land, but some live in the sea.

Example awarded 3 marks

Most snakes live on land,
but some live in the sea.

Example awarded 2 marks

Most snakes live on land, but some live in the sea.

Example awarded 1 mark

Most Snakes Live on Land, but
some Live in the sea.

Writing Test Mark Scheme

The Categories

Writing is assessed for:

Punctuation
Purpose & Organisation
Style

The mark scheme for punctuation is <u>the same</u> for all pieces of writing.

Children may develop the skills used in each category at different rates.
So, if a child is level 4 in one category, they may not be level 4 in another.

Using the Mark Scheme

First use the level descriptions below to mark the piece for punctuation. Read all the descriptions and judge which description <u>best fits</u> the child's script. Look for things which <u>do</u> fit and balance them against things that <u>don't</u> fit.

When you've decided <u>roughly</u> which level the piece is, make up your mind by looking at the descriptions of the levels above and below. The levels 3– and 5+ are included to help you with this.

Level 3– (Just below level 3) is <u>not</u> level 2 but just outside the normal level 3.
Level 5+ is <u>not</u> level 6 but outstanding work, beyond what is needed for level 5.
If the child's work <u>obviously</u> does not meet the description of a level 3–, it should be given a mark of zero.

Then find the level descriptions for Purpose & Organisation, and Style, and work out what level the piece is in each of these categories.

Finally add up the marks for all three categories to give the total Writing Test score.

All Pieces

| Stop Press! | Special Delivery | I Just Couldn't Go Home | School Hero |

| Mountain Village | Tree Lover | Lost | The Boxes |

PUNCTUATION

Level 3–	(Just below level 3) Sometimes uses capital letters and full stops in the right places. **2 marks.**
Level 3	Uses capitals, speech marks, ?, ! and full stops correctly in at least half the sentences. **4 marks.**
Level 4	Most sentences have capital letters, ?, ! and full stops used correctly. Sometimes uses commas to split up sentences (eg: for items in a list). Sometimes uses commas instead of full stops. Good use of omissive apostrophes (*don't, can't, isn't*). **5 marks.**
Level 5	Almost all sentences have capital letters, ?, ! and full stops used correctly. Uses commas, apostrophes and capitalises proper nouns in appropriate places. Uses other punctuation (eg: ( ) , –) to enhance descriptions or add humour. **6 marks.**
Level 5+	(Highest level) Uses different punctuation to clarify meaning and change pace. Commas used in sentences to divide clauses and make meaning clear. Possibly shows correct use of –, ; and : within long sentences. **7 marks.**

All Stories

Lost	The Boxes	I Couldn't Go Home	School Hero

PURPOSE & ORGANISATION

Level 3–	(Just below level 3) Writes story by narrating real or imaginary events. Some use of story structure: intro, character and two or more events in chronological order. Story language used where appropriate (eg: *One day...*, *suddenly*). **9 marks.**
Level 3	Story has simple beginning, middle and ending. Events relate to each other but may not be well paced. Includes some imaginative details for interest, suspense or humour (eg: speech or writing about setting, feelings or motives). **12 marks.**
Level 4	Coherent and well paced. Clear intro, middle and end. Events develop in a logical way. Characterisation (eg: speech). Characters interact. Lively writing and holds the reader's interest (eg: by developing events or characters). **15 marks.**
Level 5	Well structured and uses a form well (eg: realistic, adventure, fantasy). Balances dialogue, action and description. Engages interest (eg: opening story with action or dialogue, moving between places and time). Writer comments on what's happening or thoughts and feelings. Paragraphs used to divide story (opening, main events, end). **18 marks.**
Level 5+	(Highest level) Well constructed in an appropriate form. A theme (main idea) and plot are developed. Details and sequence are written confidently and sustain reader's interest (eg: using surprise, non–linear time, relationships between characters, reflection on what's happening). Paragraphs are appropriately used to organise ideas. **21 marks.**

STYLE

Level 3–	(Just below level 3) Uses spoken language structures (eg: ideas linked with *and / then / so*). Vocab may vary but mostly like speech (eg: *make, thing, have, got*). **2 marks.**
Level 3	Written style may be shown by using connectives (*but, when, because*) to show how ideas are related. May use simple adverbs or noun phrases for variety (run fast, plant pot). **4 marks.**
Level 4	Uses more complex sentences, for example, different connectives (*when, rather than, although, however*). May expand sentences before or after the noun. Chooses phrases well and uses some adventurous vocab. Pronouns and tenses are mostly consistent. **5 marks.**
Level 5	Uses simple and complex sentences well. Imaginative vocab. Language is precise and conveys writer's meaning. Matches language (colloquial, dialect or standard) to level of formality. **6 marks.**
Level 5+	(Highest level) Varies sentence structures and vocab. May use literary features (eg: alliteration) appropriate to the type of story. May use similes (*shining like a ...*), metaphors (*as big as a ...*) or dialect for characterisation. **7 marks.**

Leaflet, Interview, Letter and Diary

Mountain Village	Stop Press!	Tree Lover	Special Delivery

The **General Stuff** sections on pages 65 and 66 give general level descriptions for **Purpose & Organisation** and **Style**. They're followed by more detailed level descriptions specific to each piece.
N.B. If a certain level **isn't** given with the detailed level descriptions it's because it's **fully covered** in the **General Stuff** box.

PURPOSE & ORGANISATION — General Stuff

Level 3–	(Just below level 3) Shows some awareness of the reader but purpose may be unclear. Some use of headings, intro or conclusion. Most writing in statements. **9 marks.**
Level 3	Uses intro and points. Points are in a sensible order but some covered in too much detail or not enough. Overall balance uneven. Uses some layout conventions (eg: a main heading). **12 marks.**
Level 4	Coherent and balanced. Presents information clearly. Ideas develop in a logical way. Correctly structured - introduction, useful points and concluding phrase. **15 marks.**
Level 5	Well structured and convincing. Covers main points and balances comments. Engages reader's attention in the intro, making purpose clear. Writes a fitting ending. Uses paragraphs. **18 marks.**
Level 5+	(Highest level) Piece sustains reader's interest. Details and sequence are confidently written. Points are well chosen and ordered. Ideas are set out in paragraphs or other features. Shows sustained awareness of reader by writing intro, describing purpose, and conclusion with summary and/or final comment. Each aspect is covered in appropriate detail. **21 marks.**

Mountain Village

Level 3	Attempts to convey information and persuade. Includes details (eg: times, prices). Uses introduction and points about the village.
Level 4	Attempts to persuade (eg: by highlighting fun aspects of the village). Structured like a real leaflet. This may include direct appeal to reader (eg: '*you'll enjoy...*', '*if you need more information...*'). Subheadings may be used.
Level 5	Balances comments about specific activities, general comments and useful information (eg: opening hours, price). Engages reader (eg: emphasising features of Mountain Village). Informs and persuades reader. May use subheadings.
Level 5+	Information about the village is covered in detail.

Stop Press!

Level 3–	Some awareness of the reader (eg: indicating speaker). Some basic features (eg: greeting or closing phrase).
Level 3	Basic features of an interview are used: intro (eg: about who is being interviewed) relevant questions and answers and a closing sentence (eg: *Thanks very much, William*). Includes details (eg: names, places). Some questions may be closed (eg: *How old are you? Did you enjoy it?*) Layout makes it clear who is speaking.
Level 4	Features of an interview are used: introduces speaker, ordered questions and a suitable closing. Keeps reader interested with lively writing (eg: developing character of the interviewee through expression, opinion and then commenting on them). Covers a range of issues well. Good layout of the dialogue.
Level 5	Convincing (eg: questions progress well). Uses appropriate features of an interview. Engages reader (eg: by writing about why the interviewee is famous). Character of interviewee is developed through a series of varied questions. If the intro or conclusion are distinct from the interview, the layout clarifies this.
Level 5+	Aspects of the interviewee's views or experiences are covered in appropriate detail, including reflection on feelings and/or events. Good coverage of events, opinions etc. Conversation is convincing for the reader. Layout is fully appropriate.

Tree Lover

Level 3–	May show awareness of purpose by stating writer's views. Some basic features such as a greeting or closing signature.
Level 3	Some direct instructions or expression of opinions. Some layout conventions used (eg: *Dear Ms Doggart*).
Level 4	Adequately covers the points raised in the newspaper letter. Structured like a real letter. Conclusion may make a direct appeal to the reader (eg: *there's no need to be frightened*). Attempts to inform and persuade although not always by responding to the points in Jane's letter.
Level 5	Convincing (eg: uses info in the question). Uses appropriate features of an interview. Engages reader (eg: personal comments or referring to what follows). Points inform reader and reassure her (eg: by effectively countering Jane's points).
Level 5+	Thorough coverage of main issues. Sustained awareness of reader (eg: an intro establishing who the writer is).

Special Delivery

Level 3–	May show awareness of purpose by stating writer's views. May be written as a narrative. Pieces may not be connected.
Level 3	Simple opening to establish the context. Some expression of opinions. Details added to clarify, create interest or add humour. Writing may be in narrative form but it includes feelings or comments on importance (eg: *I feel left out, I felt so happy*). The distinction between the two pieces may not be clear.
Level 4	Events progress logically. Pieces are distinct and events are developed to give focus. Pieces may be linked by referring in the second piece to something in the first (eg: *I bet he'll have blond hair like me / I was wrong, he's got brown hair*). Comments suggest the character of the writer. Shows awareness of the reader, maybe by writing an intro outlining what's happening.
Level 5	Voice of writer is clear and sustained. Makes appeals to reader (eg: *Are you wondering what Mum called him? Well, it's... JACK!*) Clear links between the pieces, for example by commenting on feelings felt in the first piece in the second.
Level 5+	Balance between what's happening and reflection on the events. Links between pieces are explicit (eg: *He'll take Mum away from me / I was worried about him hogging Mum all the time...*) or implicit (*He'll take Mum away from me / Mum's really busy*). Refers back and forwards in time. Conventions used to separate sections and entries (eg: paragraphs).

STYLE — General Stuff

Level 3– (Just below level 3) Simple spoken language sentence structure and vocab. Shown by sentences starting with the same word (eg: *It, There is*). Connectives are absent or simple (*and, but, then*). **2 marks.**

Level 3 Connectives used to link ideas logically (eg: *also, as well, because*). Uses simple adverbs and adjectives (see examples) to add interest. Most subjects and verbs in sentences agree. **4 marks.**

Level 4 Connectives give order and emphasis or relate ideas (see examples). Chooses words for interest or to be precise (see examples). Pronouns and tenses are mostly consistent throughout. **5 marks.**

Level 5 An impersonal or passive style may be used to change focus. Level of formality is sustained and generally well chosen. Repetition is avoided using words, grouping subjects before a main verb or referring back and forwards (eg: *that, it, these*). Vocab varies, using technical and specific terms to add precision or economy (see examples). **6 marks.**

Level 5+ (Highest level) Shows control over language and uses same level of formality throughout. Vocab varies. Sentence length varies – long for explaining and short for effect. Word order changes to develop themes and keep reader's interest. **7 marks.**

Mountain Village

Level 3 Written style may be shown by, for example, directly addressing the reader or impersonal sentences (eg: *The village has...*) Simple adverbs and adjectives (eg: *a high mountain*).

Level 4 Expands sentences (eg: *the riding centre with 15 horses*) or uses subordinate clauses (eg: *the rock face, where many...*). Attempts to convey a persuasive tone (eg: *why not try your hand; these are just a few of the activities*). Connectives (eg: *if...then, to*). Chooses words for interest or to be precise (eg: *experienced staff, latest technology*).

Level 5 Vocab (eg: *adventurous, outstanding scenery, piste*).

Stop Press!

Level 3– Simple questions and answers starting with the same word (eg: *I, We*) or echoing the question without a proper answer.

Level 3 Written style may be shown by, for example, different question structures. Simple adverbs and adjectives (eg: *actually, famous*).

Level 4 Expands sentences (eg: *an expensive blue racing car*) or uses subordinate clauses (eg: *Rachael, who wrote to me...*). Avoids repetition by not repeating the question (eg: *What will your next project be? Well, it'll be something different...*) Uses devices to indicate speech (eg: *er, um, sort of*). Connectives (eg: *though, when*). Good vocab (eg: *experienced staff, latest technology, recording deal, parliament, reputation*).

Level 5 Appropriate emphasis is used in speech, such as repetition (eg: *I'm not as clever as Ben but I'm more outgoing than Georgia*). Good vocab (examples as above).

Level 5+ Word order changes (eg: *Having won the marathon, how have your ambitions changed?*). Uses language to show interviewer and interviewee as different people. Speech is convincing and the speakers react to what each other says.

Tree Lover

Level 3 Written style may be shown by, for example, generalising words to express opinion (eg: *never, always*). Simple adverbs and adjectives (eg: *pretty, strong*).

Level 4 Expands sentences (eg: *tree with silver bark*) or uses subordinate clauses (eg: *in summer, when it is hot...*). May use generalising sentences (eg: *all trees have fruit*). Connectives (eg: *if...then, [so as] to*). Good vocab (eg: *exaggerate, ancient, magnificent, habitat, photosynthesis*).

Level 5 Good vocab (examples as above).

Special Delivery

Level 3 Written style may be shown by, for example, generalising words to express opinion (eg: never, always). Simple adverbs and adjectives (eg: *pretty, strong*). Diary writing may be suggested by using some abbreviated sentences (eg: *Just got home, Can't believe it*).

Level 4 Expands sentences (eg: *a tiny person with blond hair...*) or uses subordinate clauses (eg: *After I'd told Mum, I felt happier*). Good vocab (eg: *unbearable, miniature, nervous, nursery, spitting image*). May use abbreviated sentences or conversational style appropriate to diary writing.

Level 5 Appropriate style of addressing the reader throughout. May use conversational style to create informal diary writing. Sentence structure varies and may be passive to change the focus. Good vocab (*examples as above*).

Level 5+ A conversational style may be used, sustained throughout. Creates effects, for example, feelings changing over time.

<u>*Reading Paper 1 — Answers*</u>

Section 1

1	flapping their wings **2** The larger the bird is the less it has to flap.	**4 marks**
3	hanging in the air **4** specially shaped wings	

5   2 marks for all boxes correctly filled. 1 mark for 3 or 4 boxes correctly filled. **A:** It pushes air downwards to keep it in the air.   **B & C:** It is made of light materials and is streamlined. **A:** It needs strong, powerful wings to take off. **B:** The thrust of its engine drives it forwards. **C:** It flies downwards looking for pockets of air to lift it up.
2 marks

6   1 mark for an answer which indicates that the text is about flight, eg: It's about things which can fly; It's about birds, planes and gliders.   2 marks for an answer which recognises how the writer feels about flying, eg: The writer thinks flying is wonderful; The writer thinks birds and planes are wonderful because they can fly; You need wings to fly, and flying is wonderful.
2 marks

7   1 mark for each of these reasons, maximum of 2 marks. To stop the air dragging them down; Because the engines need to lift the planes into the air; If the planes were heavy the engines would not be able to push them fast enough to make them take off.
2 marks

8   *Aeroplane*   Thrust from the engine lifts its weight.
      Glider   Pockets of rising air take it back up.
      Bird   Flaps its wings to push air down.
                   OR Air lifts bird because of specially shaped wings.
4 marks

9   1 mark for each for 2 of these: The heading is in larger writing; It is at the top of the page; There is a black box around the heading.
2 marks

10   1 mark for The seagull was still.
2 marks for any answer, even a very simple one, that refers to the author's intentions:
It's a good way of saying that the bird was still. **OR** It makes the seagull seem still. **OR** The author wanted you to think that the bird was hanging still in the air. **OR** To give you the feeling that the seagull was still.
2 marks

11   1 mark for three answers from: They have specially shaped wings (for lift). They need huge engines. They are made of light materials and are streamlined. The engines thrust the plane forwards to lift it into the air.
1 mark

12   1 mark for: The fact boxes have subheadings. **OR** They have bullet points. **OR** The boxes stand out. **OR** There aren't as many words in the boxes.
1 mark

Section 2

1	1 mark for Morning	**1 mark**
2	1 mark for one of these: To show that the plane was moving. **OR** To show that the flight had already started.	**1 mark**
3	1 mark for each answer from this list, maximum 2 marks: Landing/coming down/the flight ending **OR** feeling different **OR** the person feels happy and sad **OR** the person is thinking about the flight.	**2 marks**
4	2 marks for 4 words from this list, 1 mark for 2 or 3: twisting, climbing, swooping, rolls, diving.	**2 marks**
5	The last verse is about coming down/landing.	**1 mark**

6   1 mark for 'it is shiny/grey/gleaming'.

2 marks for any answer that mentions the author's intent. The answer can be as simple as:
It's a good way to describe something grey and shiny **OR** It makes it seem shiny like a slug's trail **OR** It tells you what the trail looks like in the sky

2 marks for answers that also say something about slug's trails that isn't mentioned in the poem, such as
It shows you that the plane's trail is winding.
2 marks

7 Happy to have been on the flight but sad it's over. | 1 mark

8 a) Patchwork is little bits/squares/shapes of cloth sewn together. | 1 mark

b) 1 mark for Fields look like patchwork from high up OR It gives an idea of how high the plane is. | 1 mark

Section 3

1 1 mark for It gives you the feeling that it's all happening right now OR It makes it more exciting/immediate. | 1 mark

2 1 mark for each set of facts correctly matched up. *Orville and Wilbur Wright* SHOULD BE LINKED TO *made the flight in December* AND *made the first flight in history.* *John Alcock and Lieutenant Arthur Whitten Brown* SHOULD BE LINKED TO *won a prize of £10 000* AND *flew for more than 16 hours.* *Louis Bleriot* SHOULD BE LINKED TO *flew from Calais to Dover* AND *damaged the plane during landing.* | 3 marks

3 3 marks for all correct. 2 marks for 3 or 4 correct. 1 mark for 2 correct.
Orville Wright made the first powered flight in history: FACT. The sea must have been dark and frightening to fly over; OPINION. What an incredible day: OPINION. The plane sometimes darted up to ten feet in the air: FACT. Alcock and Brown were national heroes: FACT. | 3 marks

4 1 mark for each of these, maximum of 2 marks: a whirling arm to launch a flying machine OR a gunpowder engine OR big flapping wings. | 2 marks

5 1 mark for each good reason, maximum 2 marks. No marks are given for the choice of word. Some example reasons are given here.
Powerful: to show that the wings were strong enough to allow a person to fly. Big/large: to show that the wings were big enough to allow a person to fly or to make them seem impressive. Streamlined: to show that the wings were like birds' wings or to show that the wings would be good at flying. | 2 marks

6 1 mark for answers that partially explain using the story, such as: Icarus tried to fly and his wings melted.
2 marks for an answer that gives a fuller explanation, such as: Icarus died and this shows that something can easily go wrong. OR Icarus tried to fly but he died because it was too dangerous. | 2 marks

Section 4

1 2 marks for all titles and writers correctly matched up. 1 mark for 2 or 3 correctly matched up.
Wonderful Wings — an ornithologist. First Flight — someone who wants to tell you how amazing flying feels. The flight of Daedalus and Icarus — someone who's not sure if people should fly. Bleriot crosses the Channel — someone writing for a newspaper. | 2 marks

2 1 mark for answers that say what the booklet says in general.
It says mainly good things about flying OR It doesn't say that flying is dangerous.
2 marks for answers with evidence from one part of the booklet.
It explains how a plane flies. If you understand how it works, it isn't as frightening OR The poem shows how exciting and fun flying is.
3 marks for answers with evidence from 2 or more parts of the booklet.
It explains how planes fly, and the poem says how exciting flying can be OR The 'Famous Fliers' part of the booklet shows that people have been flying long distances since the very early days of flying, and even in 'The Flight of Daedalus and Icarus,' Icarus only dies because he was showing off. | 3 marks

Reading Paper 2 — Answers

SECTION ONE	
1 China **2** bird cage **3** ungrateful creature **4** wouldn't let cages near the palace	4 marks
5 1 mark for: It couldn't fly any more OR It couldn't get out OR It was stuck	
2 marks for: The Emperor had trapped it against its will OR It was in a cage so it couldn't fly any more OR It was in a cage so it couldn't follow the Emperor around any more.	2 marks
6 1 mark for: He felt happy. 2 marks for: He felt at peace with the world and it made him think of hot summer days lying in the shade with a cold drink OR A similar answer using the text.	2 marks
7 The Emperor ordered his advisers to bring the nightingale to him.	1 mark
8 1 mark for each of these: He decides he is bored with his mechanical bird and he breaks it. He says he'll never keep the nightingale in the palace against its will OR Give marks for page reference eg: the middle of page 6 and the bottom of page 7.	2 marks
9 1 mark for each of these reasons, maximum of 4 marks: It sings whenever the Emperor wants it to / It never changes its song / It sings a proper tune Golden feathers are finer than real feathers / It always does what the Emperor commands	4 marks
10 The gold bird raised its head and began to sing.	1 mark
11 1 mark for 1 clue, 2 marks for 2: He is much older and frailer. He becomes ill. He is bored by the mechanical bird.	2 marks
12 1 mark for: He was sad OR He was upset OR He felt guilty	
2 marks for: He felt guilty / angry with himself because he kept it in a cage against its will OR He realised how much he enjoyed the song and felt sad he wouldn't hear it again.	2 marks
13 To describe how they waddled / what they looked like in black robes OR To make them seem funny / stupid OR To show how they were all the same, like a herd.	1 mark
14 1 mark for simple reason: YES/NO He doesn't put the nightingale in a cage. 2 marks for generalisation, using one part of the text: YES/NO He treats his advisers better when the bird comes back. YES/NO When the bird flies away, he stops taking things for granted. 3 marks for answer backed up with evidence and explaining how he's changed: YES/NO He cries when he realises that his cruelty has made the bird fly away. After that he won't allow cages near his palace to make the bird feel happier. YES/NO He is kind to the bird when it returns. He gives it water on his finger. YES/NO He stops being cruel to his advisers. At the beginning, 'his advisers were all afraid of him' but at the end, he greets them enthusiastically.	3 marks
15 At the beginning, the Emperor was the most important so his name came first. At the end, the names are swapped around to show that the nightingale is just as important.	1 mark
16 It is set in the past OR It is hard to tell if it really happened or not OR It has a message.	1 mark
17 1 mark for moral not central to the story: You shouldn't put birds in cages OR Feeling calm can make you feel better. 2 marks for moral central to the story: We shouldn't take things for granted OR Animals in cages are unhappy OR Nature is better than man–made machines. 3 marks for an explained moral or more than one: We only realise how important things are when they are gone and this shows us not to take things for granted. People can change so being able to forgive is important. OR Treating people and animals badly makes them dislike you. Putting birds in cages is wrong because it takes away their freedom.	3 marks

Reading Paper 2 — Answers

SECTION 2

1   Give 1 mark for any three facts, for example:
Some animals are dying out because their habitats are being destroyed by deforestation.
Thousands of tourists go to the Lake District every year to climb and sail.
Some animals are dying out because of hunting.
Tracks up mountains are eroded because so many people climb on them.   **1 mark**

2   1 mark for simple reason:
He thinks the people are wrong / stupid OR
He is making a point by using strong words OR He is exaggerating.
2 marks for reason with evidence:
He feels strongly that these people are wrong so he uses words to emphasise their
stupidity OR He means that they don't think ahead to the effect their actions may have OR
They are insulting words which might make people think harder about what they do.   **2 marks**

3   1 mark for simple explanation:
YES/NO   I agree with what he says OR YES   I used to think caging animals was always wrong.
2 marks for fuller explanation referring to text:
YES/NO   I agree that it's wrong to cage animals, even a mouse or rat, but I agree that
humans need to help animals that are dying out OR
YES/NO   I thought zoos were really nice places to visit but now I think that it is wrong for
them to keep animals just for us to look at.   **2 marks**

4   To highlight the name of the person being interviewed OR It is the sub-heading.   **1 mark**

5   an interview should be circled.   **1 mark**

6   An explanation of unusual/new words in an article.   **1 mark**

SECTION 3

1   1 mark for each correct similarity. Maximum 3 marks. Many possible answers – depends on which two animals are chosen. For example:
Giant pandas and rhinos both eat plants.
Zoos have breeding programmes for tigers and giant pandas.
Giant pandas and rhinos both tend to live alone.
Tigers and rhinos are both hunted – tigers for their skins and the rhino for its horns.   **3 marks**

2   Tiger   **1 mark**

3   They scare people 1 mark. They make people think of stupid horror films 1 mark.   **2 marks**

4   1 mark for a point about only one piece: Rhinoceros is facts OR The Red Wolf Returns is about feelings.
2 marks for a simple comparison: The Red Wolf Returns is more about feelings than the other piece.
3 marks for comparison describing the differences:
The Red Wolf Returns talks about how the writer feels but the piece about the rhinoceros
is mostly facts OR The Red Wolf Returns is about opinions / emotions but the piece about
rhinos is just information OR The Red Wolf Returns is positive about the wolves' survival
but the others are more negative.   **3 marks**

5   All the animals are hunted OR All the animals are in danger from poachers or people
shooting them OR All of them may become extinct without help from humans.   **1 mark**

SECTION 4

1   1 mark for a general point, for example: I liked it best because the facts were written clearly.
2 marks for one point with evidence or two points: ... because I like reading about real people and he is
really making a difference to conservation.
3 marks for points with evidence and comparisons to the other pieces:
... the writing keeps you in suspense and there is a good moral to the story. The other
pieces are mostly information so they didn't make me want to keep reading.   **3 marks**